The Art of Stillness
Adventures in Going Nowhere

PICO IYER

Photography by EYDÍS EINARSDÓTTIR

TED Books
Simon & Schuster

London   New York   Toronto   Sydney   New Delhi

TEDBooks

First published in Great Britain by Simon & Schuster UK Ltd, 2014
A CBS COMPANY

First TED Books hardcover edition November 2014

TED BOOKS and colophon are registered trademarks of TED Conferences, LLC
TED, the TED logo, and TED Books are trademarks of TED Conferences, LLC.

For information on licensing the TED talk that accompanies this book, or other
content partnerships with TED, please contact TEDBooks@TED.com.

3 5 7 9 10 8 6 4

Simon & Schuster UK Ltd
1st Floor
222 Gray's Inn Road
London WC1X 8HB

www.simonandschuster.co.uk

Simon & Schuster Australia, Sydney
Simon & Schuster India, New Delhi

A CIP catalogue record for this book is available
from the British Library

ISBN: 978-1-47113-886-7
ISBN: 978-1-47113-887-4 (ebook)

Interior design by MGMT
Jacket Design by Lewis Csizmazia
Jacket Photography by Eydís Einarsdóttir

Printed and bound by CPI Group (UK) Ltd, Croydon, CR0 4YY

For Sonny Mehta, who has taught me, and so many others,
about art, stillness, and the relation between them.

TABLE OF CONTENTS

If I ever go looking for my heart's desire again, I won't look any further than my own backyard. Because if it isn't there, I never really lost it to begin with.
—Dorothy, *The Wizard of Oz*

Introduction
Going Nowhere

The sun was scattering diamonds across the ocean as I drove toward the deserts of the east. Leonard Cohen, my hero since boyhood, was singing so long to Marianne on my sound system when I turned onto the snarl of freeways that clog and clutter central Los Angeles. The sharp winter sun disappeared behind a wall of gray for more than an hour, and then at last I drew out again into the clear.

Turning off the freeway, I followed a riddle of side streets onto a narrower road, all but empty, that snaked up into the high, dark San Gabriel Mountains. Very soon all commotion fell away. Los Angeles simplified itself into a silhouette of peaks in the distance.

High up—signs prohibiting the throwing of snowballs now appeared along the road—I came to a cluster of rough cabins scattered across a hillside. A small man in his sixties, stooped and shaven-headed, stood waiting for me in a rough parking lot. As soon as I got out of my car, he offered a deep ceremonial bow—though we'd never met before—and insisted on carrying my things into the cabin where I was to stay for the next many days. His dark and threadbare monastic robes flew around him in the wind.

Once inside the shelter of the room, the monk started cutting up some freshly baked bread, to console me for my "long drive." He put on a kettle for tea. He told me he had a wife for me if I wanted one (I didn't; I had one on the way).

I'd come up here in order to write about my host's near-silent, anonymous life on the mountain, but for the moment I lost all sense of where I was. I could hardly believe that this rabbinical-seeming gentleman in wire-rimmed glasses and wool cap was in truth the singer and poet who'd been renowned for thirty years as an international heartthrob, a constant traveler, and an Armani-clad man of the world.

Leonard Cohen had come to this Old World redoubt to make a life—an art—out of stillness. And he was working on simplifying himself as fiercely as he might on the verses of one of his songs, which he spends more than ten years polishing to perfection. The week I was visiting, he was essentially spending seven days and nights in a bare meditation hall, sitting stock-still. His name in the monastery, Jikan, referred to the silence between two thoughts.

The rest of the time he largely spent doing odd jobs around the property, cleaning dishes in the kitchen and, most of all, tending to the Japanese abbot of the Mt. Baldy Zen Center, Joshu Sasaki, then eighty-eight years old. Cohen ended up sitting still with his elderly friend for more than forty years.

One evening—four in the morning, the end of December—Cohen took time out from his meditations to walk down to my cabin and try to explain what he was doing here.

Sitting still, he said with unexpected passion, was "the real deep entertainment" he had found in his sixty-one years on the planet. "Real profound and voluptuous and delicious entertainment. The real feast that is available within this activity."

Was he kidding? Cohen is famous for his mischief and ironies.

He wasn't, I realized as he went on. "What else would I be doing?" he asked. "Would I be starting a new marriage with a young woman and raising another family? Finding new drugs, buying more expensive wine? I don't know. This seems to me the most luxurious and sumptuous response to the emptiness of my own existence."

Typically lofty and pitiless words; living on such close terms with silence clearly hadn't diminished his gift for golden sentences. But the words carried weight when coming from one who seemed to have tasted all the pleasures that the world has to offer.

Being in this remote place of stillness had nothing to do with piety or purity, he assured me; it was simply the most practical way he'd found of working through the confusion and terror that had long been his bedfellows. Sitting still with his aged Japanese friend, sipping Courvoisier, and listening to the crickets deep into the night, was the closest he'd come to finding lasting happiness, the kind that doesn't change even when life throws up one of its regular challenges and disruptions.

"Nothing touches it," Cohen said, as the light came into the cabin, of sitting still. Then he remembered himself, perhaps, and gave me a crinkly, crooked smile. "Except if you're courtin'," he added. "If you're young, the hormonal thrust has its own excitement."

Going nowhere, as Cohen described it, was the grand adventure that makes sense of everywhere else.

• • •

Sitting still as a way of falling in love with the world and everything in it; I'd seldom thought of it like that. Going nowhere as a way of cutting through the noise and finding fresh time and energy to share with others; I'd sometimes moved toward the idea, but it had never come home to me so powerfully as in the example of this man who seemed to have everything, yet found his happiness, his freedom, in giving everything up.

Late one night, as my gracious host tried to instruct me in the proper way of sitting in the lotus position—rigorous but relaxed—I couldn't find the words to tell him that I'd never been tempted to meditate. As one who'd been crossing continents alone since the age of nine, I'd always found my delight in movement; I'd even become a travel writer so that my business and my pleasure could become one.

Yet, as Cohen talked about the art of sitting still (in other words, clearing the head and stilling the emotions)—and as I observed the sense of attention, kindness, and even delight that seemed to arise out of his life of going nowhere—I began to think about how liberating it might be for any of us to give it a try. One could start just by taking a few minutes out of every day to sit quietly and do nothing, letting what moves one rise to the surface. One could take a few days out of every season to go on retreat or enjoy a long walk in the wilderness, recalling what lies deeper than the moment or the self. One could even, as Cohen was doing, try to find a life in which stage sets and performances disappear and one is reminded, at a level deeper than all words, how making a living and making a life sometimes point in opposite directions.

The idea has been around as long as humans have been, of course; the poets of East Asia, the philosophers of ancient Greece and Rome, regularly made stillness the center of their lives. But has the need for being in one place ever been as vital as it is right now? After a thirty-year study of time diaries, two sociologists found that Americans were actually working fewer hours than we did in the 1960s, but we *feel* as if we're working more. We have the sense, too often, of running at top speed and never being able to catch up.

With machines coming to seem part of our nervous systems, while increasing their speed every season, we've lost our Sundays, our weekends, our nights off—our holy days, as some would have it; our bosses, junk mailers, our parents can find us wherever we are, at any time of day or night. More and more of us feel like emergency-room physicians, permanently on call, required to heal ourselves but unable to find the prescription for all the clutter on our desk.

• • •

As I came down from the mountain, I recalled how, not many years ago, it was access to information and movement that seemed our greatest luxury; nowadays it's often freedom from information, the chance to sit still, that feels like the ultimate prize. Stillness is not just an indulgence for those with enough resources—it's a necessity for anyone who wishes to gather less visible resources. Going nowhere, as Cohen had shown me, is not about austerity so much as about coming closer to one's senses.

I'm not a member of any church, and I don't subscribe to any creed; I've never been a member of any meditation or yoga group (or any group at all, in fact). This book is simply about how one person tries to take care of his loved ones, do his job, and hold on to some direction in a madly accelerating world. It's deliberately short, so you can read it in one sitting and quickly return to your busy (perhaps overbusy) life. I don't claim to have any answers, only questions that you can deepen or open further out. But I'd been reminded on the mountain that talking about stillness is really a way of talking about clarity and sanity and the joys that endure. Take this book, about these unexpected pleasures, as an invitation to the adventure of going nowhere.

1 Passage to Nowhere

When I was twenty-nine, I had the life I might have dreamed of as a boy: a twenty-fifth-floor office in Midtown Manhattan, four blocks from Times Square; an apartment on Park Avenue and Twentieth Street; the most interesting and convivial colleagues I could imagine; and an endlessly fascinating job writing about world affairs—the ending of apartheid in South Africa, the People Power Revolution in the Philippines, the turmoil around Indira Gandhi's assassination—for *Time* magazine. I had no dependents or responsibilities, and I could—and did—take long vacations everywhere from Bali to El Salvador.

For all the daily excitement, however, something inside me felt that I was racing around so much that I never had a chance to see where I was going, or to check whether I was truly happy. Indeed, hurrying around in search of contentment seemed a perfect way of ensuring I'd never be settled or content. Too often I reminded myself of someone going on and on about world peace in the most contentious and divisive of terms.

So I decided to leave my dream life and spend a year in a small, single room on the backstreets of the ancient Japanese capital of Kyoto. I couldn't have said exactly why I was doing this except that I felt I had enjoyed a wonderful diet of movement and stimulation in New York, and now it was time to balance that out with something simpler, and learn how to make those joys less external and ephemeral.

As soon as I left the security of my job and plunged into the unknown, my father began calling me up, unsurprisingly concerned, to berate me for being a "pseudoretiree." I couldn't blame him; all the institutions of higher skepticism to which he'd so generously sent me had insisted that the point of life was to get somewhere in the world, not to go nowhere. But the nowhere I was interested in had more corners and dimensions than I could possibly express to him (or myself), and somehow seemed larger and more unfathomable than the endlessly diverting life I'd known in the city; it opened onto a landscape as vast as those of the Morocco and Indonesia and Brazil I had come to know, combined.

I thought back to the day I'd wandered through an exhibition of Mark Rothko abstracts and felt myself drawn beneath the surface to a stillness that seemed bottomless and rich with every color; I recalled the time a friend had told me how John Cage had unearthed symphonies in the silences he'd set up in jam-packed auditoria. More than that, I'd long been moved by the way Thomas Merton, gregarious traveler, heavy drinker, and wounded lover, had stepped into a Trappist monastery in Kentucky and become Father Louis, taking his restlessness in a less visible direction.

Going nowhere, as Leonard Cohen would later emphasize for me, isn't about turning your back on the world; it's about stepping away now and then so that you can see the world more clearly and love it more deeply.

• • •

The idea behind Nowhere—choosing to sit still long enough to turn inward—is at heart a simple one. If your car is broken, you don't try to find ways to repaint its chassis; most of our problems—and therefore our solutions, our peace of mind—lie within. To hurry around trying to find happiness outside ourselves makes about as much sense as the comical figure in the Islamic parable who, having lost a key in his living room, goes out into the street to look for it because there's more light there. As Epictetus and Marcus Aurelius reminded us more than two millennia ago, it's not our experiences that form us but the ways in which we respond to them; a hurricane sweeps through town, reducing everything to rubble, and one man sees it as a liberation, a chance to start anew, while another, perhaps even his brother, is traumatized for life. "There is nothing either good or bad," as Shakespeare wrote in *Hamlet*, "but thinking makes it so."

So much of our lives takes place in our heads—in memory or imagination, in speculation or interpretation—that sometimes I feel that I can best change my life by changing the way I look at it. As America's wisest psychologist, William James, reminded us, "The greatest weapon against stress is our ability to choose one thought over another." It's the perspective we choose—not the places we visit—that ultimately tells us where we stand. Every time I take a trip, the experience acquires meaning and grows deeper only after I get back home and, sitting still, begin to convert the sights I've seen into lasting insights.

• • •

This isn't to suggest that travel is useless; I've often known stillness most fruitfully in a sunlit corner of Ethiopia or Havana. It's just a reminder that it's not the physical movement that carries us up so much as the spirit we bring to it. As Henry David Thoreau, one of the great explorers of his time, reminded himself in his journal, "It matters not where or how far you travel—the farther commonly the worse—but how much alive you are."

Two years after my year in Japan, I took some more concerted steps in the direction of Nowhere. Kyoto had given me a taste of stillness, but still I had to support myself by traveling, and in the previous few months I'd been lucky enough to journey all across Argentina, down to Tierra del Fuego, and then to China and Tibet and North Korea. I'd been twice in successive months to London and Paris, returning regularly to visit my mother in California. I had long, exciting voyages around Vietnam and Iceland coming up and felt more than spoiled for choice, able to refresh my engagement with the world every few weeks. But at some point all the horizontal trips in the world can't compensate for the need to go deep into somewhere challenging and unexpected. Movement makes richest sense when set within a frame of stillness.

So I got into my car and followed a road north along the California coast from my mother's house, and then drove up an even narrower path to a Benedictine retreat house a friend had told me about. When I got out of my worn and dust-streaked white Plymouth Horizon, it was to step into a thrumming, crystal silence. And when I walked into the little room where I was to spend three nights, I couldn't begin to remember any of the arguments I'd been thrashing out in my head on the way up, the phone calls that had seemed so urgent when I left home. Instead, I was nowhere but in this room, with long windows looking out upon the sea.

A fox alighted on the splintered fence outside, and I couldn't stop watching, transfixed. A deer began grazing just outside my window, and it felt like a small miracle stepping into my life. Bells tolled far above, and I thought I was listening to the "Hallelujah Chorus."

I'd have laughed at such sentiments even a day before. And as soon as I went to vigils in the chapel, the spell was broken; the silence was much more tonic than any words could be. But what I discovered, almost instantly, was that as soon as I was in one place, undistracted, the world lit up and I was as happy as when I forgot about myself. Heaven is the place where you think of nowhere else.

It was a little like being called back to somewhere I knew, though I'd never seen the place before. As the monks would have told me—though I never asked them—finding what feels like real life, that change-less and inarguable something behind all our shifting thoughts, is less a discovery than a recollection.

I was so moved that, before I left, I made a reserva-tion to come back, and then again, for two whole weeks. Very soon, stepping into stillness became my sustaining luxury. I couldn't stay in the hermitage forever—I wasn't good at settling down, and I'm not part of any spiritual order—but I did feel that spending time in silence gave everything else in my days fresh value and excitement. It felt as if I was slipping out of my life and ascending a small hill from which I could make out a wider land-scape.

It was also pure joy, often, in part because I was so fully in the room in which I sat, reading the words of every book as though I'd written them. The people I met in the retreat house—bankers and teachers and real estate salespeople—were all there for much the same rea-son I was, and so seemed to be my kin, as fellow travelers elsewhere did not. When I drove back into my day-to-day existence, I felt the liberation of not needing to take my thoughts, my ambitions—my self—so seriously.

This small taste of silence was so radical and so un-like most of what I normally felt that I decided to try to change my life a little more. The year after I discovered what a transformation it could be to sit still, I moved to Japan for good—to a doll's house apartment in which my wife and I have no car, no bicycle, no bedroom or TV I can understand. I still have to support my family and keep up with the world as a travel writer and journalist, but the freedom from distraction and complication means that every day, when I wake up, looks like a clear meadow with nothing ahead of me, stretching towards the mountains.

This isn't everyone's notion of delight; maybe you have to taste quite a few of the alternatives to see the point in stillness. But when friends ask me for suggestions about where to go on vacation, I'll sometimes ask if they want to try Nowhere, especially if they don't want to have to deal with visas and injections and long lines at the airport. One of the beauties of Nowhere is that you never know where you'll end up when you head in its direction, and though the horizon is unlimited, you may have very little sense of what you'll see along the way. The deeper blessing—as Leonard Cohen had so movingly shown me, sitting still—is that it can get you as wide-awake, exhilarated, and pumping-hearted as when you are in love.

2 The Charting of Stillness

Writers, of course, are obliged by our professions to spend much of our time going nowhere. Our creations come not when we're out in the world, gathering impressions, but when we're sitting still, turning those impressions into sentences. Our job, you could say, is to turn, through stillness, a life of movement into art. Sitting still is our workplace, sometimes our battlefield.

At the blond wood child's desk where I write in Japan, I have one constant companion, and he is alight with stories about glittery parties and the war, about ravishing beauties and society hostesses and bejeweled nights at the opera. But Marcel Proust could bring this thronged world home to me only by sitting still in a cork-lined room, nearly alone, for years on end, exploring the ways in which we remake the world in more permanent form in our heads.

That, in fact, was the idea behind his epic novel, the title of which is sometimes rendered as *Remembrance of Things Past*. We glimpse a stranger in the street, and the exchange lasts barely a moment. But then we go home and think on it and think on it and try to understand what the glance meant and inspect it from this angle and from that one, spinning futures and fantasies around it. The experience that lasted an instant plays out for a lifetime inside us. It becomes, in fact, the story of our lives.

My other loyal companion in Japan, as he has been since I was a teenager traveling from Dharamsala to Bogotá and Barbados, is, as it happens, the roaming troubadour whose debut album had featured four songs with the word "travel" at their center. The first song Leonard Cohen ever delivered in public was about a man taking out an old train schedule, a highway "curling up like smoke above his shoulder." One of the most heartfelt numbers on that maiden record found him saying good-bye to a woman because he had to "wander in my time."

Leonard Cohen had become the poet laureate of those on the road, refusing to stick to any form of settling down, a "gypsy boy" who wouldn't sit still within any of the expectations we brought to him. But, like many a wanderer, he seemed always to know that it's only when you stop moving that you can be moved in some far deeper way ("Now I know why many men have stopped and wept," he writes in an early poem, "Halfway between the loves they leave and seek, / And wondered if travel leads them anywhere").

Whenever he took his pulse most directly, he tended to acknowledge that his greatest journeys were inner ones. "I needed so much to have nothing to touch," he confesses in one typically unflinching song about going to the Zen Center. "I've always been greedy that way."

• • •

Almost a decade after my first visit to Leonard Cohen's perch in the bare hall near the top of the mountain, I ran into another unlikely maverick, this time in Zürich. I was in the Hallenstadion, a thirteen-thousand-seat auditorium recently visited by Britney Spears, where the Fourteenth Dalai Lama, on whose global movements I was writing, was delivering a complex discourse on the Bodhisattva's way of life, explaining why some humans who attain Nirvana (the word means "blown out" in Sanskrit) choose to come back to the world to help the rest of us.

Many of the native English speakers there—mostly Buddhist, as I am not—were trying, if they could, to follow the intricate philosophical teachings in French, in part because the Dalai Lama's words came through his French translator with such lucid transparency. The translator's name was Matthieu Ricard, and he'd received his PhD in molecular biology from the Institut Pasteur, studying under the Nobel Prize winner François Jacob. Indeed, Matthieu's father, Jean-François Revel, was celebrated as one of France's leading intellectuals, the longtime editor of *L'Express*; his mother, Yahne le Toumelin, was well known for her abstract art. Around the family dinner table, while Matthieu was growing up, sat Buñuel and Stravinsky and Cartier-Bresson.

But when he was twenty-one, Ricard took a trip to

Nepal, and the joy and sense of discernment he'd encountered in and through some Tibetan lamas there
had so profoundly moved him that, five years on, he
abandoned his promising career in science and went
to live in the shadow of the Himalayas. He learned Tibetan, took on monastic robes, and served—for more
than a dozen years—as attendant and student of the
Tibetan teacher Dilgo Khyentse Rinpoche. At one point
in the mid-1990s, Matthieu's father flew to Nepal to
spend ten days in dialogue with his scientist son to find
out why his offspring would write (much as Leonard
Cohen might) that "Simplifying one's life to extract its
quintessence is the most rewarding of all the pursuits I
have undertaken."

The book that arose out of their discussions, *The
Monk and the Philosopher*, sold almost half a million
copies in France, in part because Ricard was able to
argue for the Buddhist "science of mind" he had taken
on with all the Cartesian clarity and eloquence he'd no
doubt inherited from his father. No one I'd met could
better explain, for example, how getting caught up in
the world and expecting to find happiness there made
about as much sense as reaching into a fire and hoping
not to get burned.

Just before I met him, Ricard had been the first par-
ticipant in an experiment conducted by researchers at
the University of Wisconsin. Scientists had attached
256 electrodes to the skulls of hundreds of volun-
teers and put them through a three-and-a-half-hour

continuous functional MRI scan to test for positive emotions (and, in later experiments, compassion, the ability to control emotional responses, the capacity to process information). The subjects were similar in every respect except that some had given themselves over to a regular practice of stillness and the others had not. Ricard's score for positive emotions was so far beyond the average of nonmonastic subjects that the researchers, after testing many others who had meditated for ten thousand hours or more and many who had not, felt obliged to conclude that those who had sat still for years had achieved a level of happiness that was, quite literally, off the charts, unseen before in the neurological literature.

By the time we met in Zürich, the fifty-nine-year-old Frenchman was routinely described as "the happiest man in the world." He was also in constant demand, explaining how happiness can be developed just as any muscle can be at the World Economic Forum in Davos, participating in conferences between scientists of matter and of mind in India, translating for the Dalai Lama across the globe, bringing the priorities he'd sharpened in stillness to the construction of clinics and schools and bridges across Tibet. Soon after we first got to know each other, I asked him a typical traveler's question: How did he deal with jet lag? He looked at me, surprised. "For me a flight is just a brief retreat in the sky," Matthieu said, as if amazed that the idea didn't strike everyone. "There's nothing I can do, so it's really quite liberating. There's nowhere else I can be. So I just sit and watch the clouds and the blue sky. Everything is still and everything is moving. It's beautiful." Clouds and blue sky, of course, are how Buddhists explain the nature of our mind: there may be clouds passing across it, but that doesn't mean a blue sky isn't always there behind the obscurations. All you need is the patience to sit still until the blue shows up again.

His explanation made a different kind of sense a few years later, when Ricard published a book of photographs that looked to me like the ultimate travel book. He'd been on retreat in a cabin on top of a mountain in Nepal for the better part of a year, and once or twice a week, he'd stepped outside and taken a picture of what lay beyond his front door. The same view, more or less, but as it changed with clouds or rain, in winter or in spring, and as the moods of the man behind the lens changed.

When I paged through the book, I realized Matthieu had inherited his mother's eye for the art of stillness as well as his father's analytical mind; these Portraits of Nowhere, as they could have been called, were magical. I saw Indonesia and Peru, sunlit valleys and storm-blackened skies in his work; it felt as if most of the world had made a house call to his cabin. The book, which he called *Motionless Journey*, might almost have been an investigation into how everything changes and doesn't change at all—how the same place looks different even as you're not really going anywhere.

But what made it most haunting was that, at heart, it was a description of an inner landscape. This is what your mind—your life—looks like when you're going nowhere. Always full of new colors, sights, and beauties; always, more or less, unaltered.

3 Alone in the Dark

None of us, of course, would want to be in a Nowhere we hadn't chosen, as prisoners or invalids are. Whenever I travel to North Korea or Yemen—to any of the world's closed or impoverished places—I see how almost anyone born to them would long to be anywhere else, and to visit other countries with the freedom that some of the rest of us enjoy. From San Quentin to New Delhi, the incarcerated are taught meditation, but only so they can see that within their confinement there may be spots of liberation. Otherwise, those in solitary may find themselves bombarded by the terrors and unearthly visitations that Emily Dickinson knew in her "still—Volcano—Life."

I once went into the woods of Alberta and sat in a cabin day after day with letters from Dickinson, the poet famous for seldom leaving her home. Her passion shook me till I had to look away, the feeling was so intense and caged; her words were explosives in a jewel box. I imagined standing with the woman in white at her window, watching her brother with his young wife, Susan—to whom Dickinson addressed some of her most passionate letters ("Oh my darling one"; "my heart is full of you, none other than you is in my thoughts")—in the house they shared one hundred yards away, across the garden.

I felt her slipping through her parlor while her brother conducted an adulterous affair in the next room, betraying the Sue they both adored. I saw her crafting, in a fury, her enflamed letters to her "Master," the atmosphere charged around her in her solitude, or writing, "I see thee better—in the Dark."

She could feel Death calling for her in her bed, she wrote, as she plumbed the shadows within the stillness; again and again she imagined herself posthumous, mourners "treading—treading" in her brain. She knew that you do not have to be a chamber to be haunted, that "Ourself behind ourself concealed— / Should startle most." Her unsettling words brought to mind poor Herman Melville, conjuring up at the same time his own version of a motionless ghost, Bartleby, a well-spoken corpse conducting a makeshift Occupy Wall Street resistance by sitting in a lawyer's office in lower Manhattan, "preferring" not to go anywhere.

Nowhere can be scary, even if it's a destination you've chosen; there's nowhere to hide there. Being locked inside your head can drive you mad or leave you with a devil who tells you to stay at home and stay at home till you are so trapped inside your thoughts that you can't step out or summon the power of intention.

A life of stillness can sometimes lead not to art but to doubt or dereliction; anyone who longs to see the light is signing on for many long nights alone in the dark. Visiting a monastery, I also realized how easy it might be to go there as an escape, or in the throes of an infatuation certain not to last. As in any love affair, the early days of a romance with stillness give little sign of the hard work to come.

Sometimes, when I returned to my monastery in midwinter, the weather was foul as I pulled up. The rain pattered down on the tin roof of my trailer throughout the night. The view through the picture windows was of nothing but mist. I didn't see or hear a living soul for days on end, and my time felt like a trial, a penitential exercise in loneliness. The downpour was so unending that I couldn't go out, and so I sat in the fog, stuck and miserable, reminded how the external environment can too easily be a reflection of—sometimes a catalyst for—an inner one.

"The way of contemplation is not even a way," as Thomas Merton, the eloquent monk, put it, "and if one follows it, what he finds is nothing." One of the laws of sitting still, in fact, is that "if you enter it with the set purpose of seeking contemplation, or, worse still, happiness, you will find neither. For neither can be found unless it is first in some sense renounced." This was all a bit paradoxical—as hard to disentangle as a Zen koan—but I could catch the fundamental point: a man sitting still is alone, often, with the memory of all he doesn't have. And what he does have can look very much like nothing.

• • •

One morning in early summer, when I was visiting Louisville, Kentucky, a new friend offered to drive me out to see the monastery where Thomas Merton had lived for more than a quarter of a century. Very soon the city was far behind us, and we were passing empty green fields and the occasional house with a cross (or words from the Bible) outside it. When we got to the place Merton had made so famous—a place that looked grave and forbidding, like a dark Victorian asylum for the mentally troubled—a tall, quiet monk who had studied under Merton offered to show us the hermitage where Father Louis (as Merton was still known there) had spent much of his last two years, having found even the monastery too full of distraction and commotion.

We walked past graves and across a field. "For the last three years," said the monk, fresh and quickly striding though in his early seventies, "I've been in love." He paused. "With a woman named Emily Dickinson."

We let this pass, and followed the man in robes to a rather rickety little cabin "in the shadow of a big cedar cross," as Merton had described it, a barn adjoining it and a tiny porch with a single chair in front of it.

Inside, the place was modestly furnished, though spacious by monastic standards. Our tour guide sat down and proceeded to recite some lines from Rainer Maria Rilke. "Always there is World," the German poet put it, "and never Nowhere without the No: that pure unseparated element which one breathes without desire and endlessly *knows*."

Then, from Dickinson:

The Brain—is wider than the Sky—
For—put them side by side—
The one the other will contain
With ease—and You—beside—

Then he got up and picked out a book at random from the shelves. "I like to read something from Father Louis's journals whenever I show people this place," the monk said. "To bring his spirit into our company. So we can feel he's here."

He opened to a random page and began to read.

"We ate herring and ham (not very much eating!) and drank our wine and read poems and talked of ourselves and mostly made love and love and love for five hours. Though we had over and over reassured ourselves and agreed that our love would have to continue always chaste and this sacrifice was essential, yet in the end we were getting rather sexy. Yet really, instead of being all wrong, it seemed eminently right. We now love with our whole bodies anyway, and I have the complete feel of her being (except her sex) as completely me."

It was a passage from Volume 5 of the printed journals, perhaps the most startling section of the sometimes angry monk's meditations. At fifty-one, Merton had gone into St. Joseph's Hospital in Louisville for back surgery. He'd scorned the trip in advance—"I do not expect much help from doctors and their damned pills"—and, the morning before he left, he wrote, as if to reassure

himself, "I am just beginning to get grounded in solitude." His one regret, should he die, he wrote, would be
the "loss of the years of solitude that might be possible."
But while in the hospital, he very quickly—after almost
a quarter-century out of the world—fell tumultuously in
love with the "very friendly and devoted" twenty-year-
old student nurse who was helping to take care of him.

The hundreds of pages in his diary in which he
thrashed out his feelings for her are agonizing to read;
it's as if this wise man who knew so much about stillness
and truth became an adolescent boy again, twisting and
turning on his bed as he tried to sort out a kind of love he
hadn't known since taking a vow of chastity. He started
bombarding the young woman with letters and naked
entreaties, made unlicensed phone calls to her from the
cellarer's office while his brother monks were at dinner.
When another monk overheard him, he confessed to his
long-suffering abbot ("about the phone calls *only*!"), but
still kept talking of forfeiting his vocation to run away
with "M." and live with her on an island.

"I am flooded with peace (whereas last Sunday the
mere idea that this might happen tore me with anguish
and panic)," Merton wrote. "I have surrendered again
to a kind of inimical womanly wisdom in M. which in-
stinctively seeks out the wound in me that most needs
her sweetness and lavishes all her love upon me there.
Instead of feeling impure, I feel purified (which is in fact
what I myself wrote the other day in the "Seven Words"
for Ned O'Gorman). I feel that somehow my sexuality

has been made real and decent again after years of rather frantic suppression (for though I thought I had it all truly controlled, this was an illusion)."

Our monk, to his credit, kept reading the passage to its end, never faltering or deciding that some other passage might be more profitable. Just one year before meeting "M.," ecstatic in his new hermitage, Merton had written, "I had decided to marry the silence of the forest. The sweet dark warmth of the whole world will have to be my wife." That, too, seemed to have changed, like the skies in Matthieu Ricard's photos. You don't get over the shadows inside you simply by walking away from them.

4 Stillness Where It's Needed Most

The idea of going nowhere is, as mentioned, as universal as the law of gravity; that's why wise souls from every tradition have spoken of it. "All the unhappiness of men," the seventeenth-century French mathematician and philosopher Blaise Pascal famously noted, "arises from one simple fact: that they cannot sit quietly in their chamber." After Admiral Richard E. Byrd spent nearly five months alone in a shack in the Antarctic, in temperatures that sank to 70 degrees below zero, he emerged convinced that "Half the confusion in the world comes from not knowing how little we need." Or, as they sometimes say around Kyoto, "Don't just do something. Sit there."

Yet the days of Pascal and even Admiral Byrd seem positively tranquil by today's standards. The amount of data humanity will collect while you're reading this book is five times greater than the amount that exists in the entire Library of Congress. Anyone reading this book will take in as much information today as Shakespeare took in over a lifetime. Researchers in the new field of interruption science have found that it takes an average of twenty-five minutes to recover from a phone call. Yet such interruptions come every eleven minutes—which means we're never caught up with our lives.

And the more facts come streaming in on us, the less time we have to process any one of them. The one thing technology doesn't provide us with is a sense of how to make the best use of technology. Put another way, the ability to gather information, which used to be so crucial, is now far less important than the ability to sift through it.

It's easy to feel as if we're standing two inches away from a huge canvas that's noisy and crowded and changing with every microsecond. It's only by stepping farther back and standing still that we can begin to see what that canvas (which is our life) really means, and to take in the larger picture.

● ● ●

As I travel the world, one of the greatest surprises I have encountered has been that the people who seem wisest about the necessity of placing limits on the newest technologies are, often, precisely the ones who helped develop those technologies, which have bulldozed over so many of the limits of old. The very people, in short, who have worked to speed up the world are the same ones most sensitive to the virtue of slowing down.

One day I visited Google's headquaters to give a talk on the Dalai Lama book I'd completed and, like most visitors, was much impressed by the trampolines, the indoor tree houses, and the workers at the time enjoying a fifth of their working hours free, letting their minds wander off leash to where inspiration might be hiding.

But what impressed me even more were the two people who greeted me as I waited for my digital ID: the Chief Evangelist for Google+, as his business card would have it, a bright-eyed, visibly spirited young soul from India who was setting up a "Yogler" program whereby the many Googlers who practice yoga could actually be trained to teach it; and the seasoned software engineer beside him who ran a celebrated and popular seven-week program called "Search Inside Yourself," whose curriculum had shown more than a thousand Googlers the quantifiable, scientific evidence that meditation could lead not just to clearer thinking and better health but to emotional intelligence.

A self-selecting pair, no doubt; these were the kind of guys who wanted to hear about the Dalai Lama. Every company has its own chief evangelists, eager to share their illuminations. But I was struck by how often Gopi, the founder of the Yogler program, spoke of how easy it was, day or night, to go into a conference room and close his eyes. It sounded a bit like Dickinson again:

The Outer—from the Inner
Derives its Magnitude—
'Tis Duke, or Dwarf, according
As is the Central Mood.

Many in Silicon Valley observe an "Internet Sabbath" every week, during which they turn off most of their devices from, say, Friday night to Monday morning, if only to regather the sense of proportion and direction they'll need for when they go back online. I was reminded of this by Kevin Kelly, one of the most passionate spokesmen for new technologies (and the founding executive editor of *Wired* magazine), who had written his latest book about how technology can "expand our individual potential" while living without a smartphone, a laptop, or a TV in his home. Kevin still takes off on months-long trips through Asian villages without a computer, so as to be rooted in the nonvirtual world. "I continue to keep the cornucopia of technology at arm's length," he writes, "so that I can more easily remember who I am."

There is now a meditation room in every building on the General Mills campus in Minneapolis, and Congressman Tim Ryan leads his colleagues in the House of Representatives in sessions of sitting still, reminding them that, if nothing else, it's been found by scientists that meditation can lower blood pressure, help boost our immune system, and even change the architecture of our brains. This has no more to do with religion or any other kind of doctrine than a trip to the (mental) health club might.

Indeed, fully a third of American companies now have "stress-reduction programs," and the number is increasing by the day—in part because workers find unclogging their minds' arteries to be so exhilarating. More than 30 percent of those enrolled in such a program at Aetna, the giant heath-care company, saw their levels of stress dropping by a third after only an hour of yoga each week. The computer chip maker Intel experimented with a "Quiet Period" of four hours every Tuesday, during which three hundred engineers and managers were asked to turn off their e-mail and phones and put up "Do Not Disturb" signs on their office doors in order to make space for "thinking time." The response proved so enthusiastic that the company inaugurated an eight-week program to encourage clearer thinking. At General Mills, 80 percent of senior executives reported a positive change in their ability to make decisions, and 89 percent said that they had become better listeners, after a similar seven-week program. Such developments are saving American corporations three hundred billion dollars a year; more important, they're a form of preemptive medicine at a time when the World Health Organization has been widely quoted as stating that "stress will be the health epidemic of the twenty-first century."

It can be strange to see mind training—going nowhere, in effect—being brought to such forward-pushing worlds; the businesses that view retreats as the best way to advance may simply be deploying new and imaginative means to the same unelevated ends. To me, the point of sitting still is that it helps you see through the very idea of pushing forward; indeed, it strips you of yourself, as of a coat of armor, by leading you into a place where you're defined by something larger. If it does have benefits, they lie within some invisible account with a high interest rate but very long-term yields, to be drawn upon at that moment, surely inevitable, when a doctor walks into your room, shaking his head, or another car veers in front of yours, and all you have to draw upon is what you've collected in your deeper moments. But there's no questioning the need for clarity and focus, especially when the stakes are highest.

One spring morning, I heard a knock on my door in the monastery that had become my secret home—located only a couple of hours' drive from Silicon Valley—and opened it up to find two young friends I'd never met before but had come to know a little through correspondence. Emma was the associate director of a research center at Stanford, and her fiancé (now husband), Andrew, was a Marine. We walked down to a small bench overlooking the blue expanse of the Pacific—no islands in front of us, no oil rigs, no whales—and Emma explained how, as a postdoc in Wisconsin, she'd spent a year raising money to fund a study to see if military veterans facing the possibility of posttraumatic stress disorder could be helped by some training in stillness.

The guys who came into her lab, she said, were—as I would expect—hard-drinking, tattoo-covered, motorbike-riding Midwestern men who had no interest at all in what they called "hippie dipshit." As far as they were concerned, she was the one being tested, not they. But then she put ten of them through a weeklong yoga-based breathing program. And when they came out of the twenty-five-hour course in going nowhere, the veterans reported significant decreases in symptoms of stress, feelings of anxiety, and even respiration rate. The ten who didn't receive the training were unchanged.

As a professional scientist, she trusted only what could be empirically backed up, so she checked the veterans' startle reflex—unusually powerful, as a rule, in hypervigilant veterans and often the cause of sleeplessness and exaggerated fear responses—and discovered that the figures chimed exactly with the veterans' subjective accounts to her. More than one of them had taken her aback by saying she had literally brought him back from the dead. She tested her sample group a second time a week after the program—and then again a year later—and the improvements held up. Her paper describing the pilot study had been peer-reviewed and accepted by the *Journal of Traumatic Stress*.

Then Andrew spoke. He remained where he was, straight-backed and alert, standing beside the bench on which Emma and I were sitting, and began by confessing, with a polite smile, that meditation practice was never going to be an easy sell in the "alpha-male, hypermacho" world of the Marine Corps. In fact, when he'd embarked upon his own very strict forty-day program in sitting still, "I was more out to prove it wrong, or just to be my disciplined Marine self and see the mission through." But soon, to his surprise, he found his hours of concentrated attention were making him unusually happy, to the point where he began to worry he was losing his edge.

His adviser assured him that he was no less alert than before, just more selective about the "potential threats or targets to respond to. Which allowed me," Andrew went on, "to ignore many of the things I would normally pay attention to and to enjoy daily life more instead." He was amazed, as a hard-charging Marine Corps Scout Sniper, "that something this simple could be so powerful. And something so soft could also make me so much harder as a Marine."

Once, he said, a buddy of his had been the officer in charge in the last Humvee in a convoy in Afghanistan. The vehicle rolled over an explosive device, and the lower parts of both the man's legs had been instantly destroyed. But—thanks to his training in "tactical breathing"—the officer had found the presence of mind to check on the others around him, to ask his driver to signal for help, and, remarkably, to tourniquet what remained of his legs and keep them propped up until help could arrive. By altering his breathing and keeping still, according to a system he'd read about in a book for active service members, he'd saved his own life and those of many around him.

No one could say it was a panacea, and I have never been one for New Age ideas. It was the ideas of old age—or at least of those whose thoughts had stood the test of time for centuries, even millennia—that carried more authority for me. But twenty-two veterans are taking their own lives around us every day, and their average age is twenty-five. It doesn't seem crazy to think that training minds might help save lives at least as much as training bodies does.

5 A Secular Sabbath

The need for an empty space, a pause, is something we have all felt in our bones; it's the rest in a piece of music that gives it resonance and shape. That's the reason American football players prefer to go into a huddle rather than just race toward the line of scrimmage, the reason a certain kind of writer will include a lot of blank space on a page, so his sentences have room to breathe (and his readers, too). The one word for which the adjective "holy" is used in the Ten Commandments is Sabbath.

In the book of Numbers, God actually condemns to death a man found collecting wood on the Sabbath. The book on the Sabbath is the longest one in the Torah, as Judith Shulevitz explains in her fine work, *The Sabbath World*. Another part of the Torah, dealing with the Sabbath's boundaries, takes up 105 pages more.

Keeping the Sabbath—doing nothing for a while—is one of the hardest things in life for me; I'd much rather give up meat or wine or sex than the ability to check my e-mails or get on with my work when I want to. If I don't answer my messages today, I tell myself, there will only be more to answer tomorrow (though, in truth, refraining from sending messages will likely diminish the number I receive); if I take time off, I somehow believe, I'll be that much more hurried the rest of the time.

Whenever I finally force myself away from my desk for a day, of course, I find the opposite: the more time I spend away from my work, the better that work will be, most often.

One day Mahatma Gandhi was said to have woken up and told those around him, "This is going to be a very busy day. I won't be able to meditate for an hour." His friends were taken aback at this rare break from his discipline. "I'll have to meditate for two," he spelled out.

I mentioned this once on a radio program and a woman called in, understandably impatient. "It's all very well for a male travel writer in Santa Barbara to talk about taking time off," she said. "But what about me? I'm a mother trying to start a small business, and I don't have the luxury of meditating for two hours a day." Yet it's precisely those who are busiest, I wanted to tell her, who most need to give themselves a break. Stress is contagious, studies have found. If only the poor, overburdened mother could ask her husband—or her mother or a friend—to look after her kids for thirty minutes a day, I'm sure she'd have much more freshness and delight to share with her children when she came back, and with her business.

Some people, if they can afford it, try to acquire a place in the country or a second home; I've always thought it easier to make a second house in the week—especially if, like most of us, you lack the funds for expensive real estate. These days, in the age of movement and connection, space, as Marx had it in another context, has been annihilated by time; we feel as though we can make contact with almost anywhere at any moment. But as fast as geography is coming under our control, the clock is exerting more and more tyranny over us. And the more we can contact others, the more, it sometimes seems, we lose contact with ourselves. When I left New York City for the backstreets of Japan, I figured I'd be growing poorer in terms of money, amusements, social life, and obvious prospects, but I'd be richer in what I prize most: days and hours.

This is what the principle of the Sabbath enshrines. It is, as Abraham Joshua Heschel, the great Jewish theologian of the last century, had it, "a cathedral in time rather than in space"; the one day a week we take off becomes a vast empty space through which we can wander, without agenda, as through the light-filled passageways of Notre Dame. Of course, for a religious person, it's also very much about community and ritual and refreshing one's relationship with God and ages past. But even for the rest of us, it's like a retreat house that ensures we'll have something bright and purposeful to carry back into the other six days.

The Sabbath recalls to us that, in the end, all our journeys have to bring us home. And we do not have to travel far to get away from our less considered habits. The places that move us most deeply, as I found in the monastery, are often the ones we recognize like long-lost

friends; we come to them with a piercing sense of famil-
iarity, as if returning to some source we already know.
"Some keep the Sabbath going to Church—" Emily Dickinson wrote. "I keep it, staying at Home."

●   ●   ●

One day, a year after meeting Matthieu Ricard and hear-
ing how a transatlantic flight could be a "retreat in the
sky," I found myself on such a flight, from Frankfurt to
Los Angeles. The woman who came and sat next to me
was young, very attractive and, as I would learn, from
Germany. As she settled into her seat, she exchanged a
few friendly words and then proceeded to sit in silence,
doing nothing, for the next twelve hours.

I slept and paged through a novel, squeezed past her to
go to the bathroom, and scrolled through options on the
monitor before me, but she just sat there, never nodding
off, yet apparently very much at peace. After we com-
menced our descent, I finally summoned the courage to
ask her if she lived in LA.

No, she said, she was a social worker, and her job was
exhausting. Now she was on her way to five weeks of vacation in Hawaii, the perfect antidote to her life in Berlin.
But she liked to use the flight over to begin to get all the
stress out of her system so that she could arrive on the
islands in as clear a state as possible, ready to enjoy her
days of rest.

I was humbled. So often I see vacations as just a way
to direct my work habits and relentlessness toward

mapping out schedules and organizing train tickets, less concerned with the quality of my time than the quantity. A flight for me had always been a chance to catch up on job-related reading, to see movies I'd never been tempted to see when they were playing at the Cineplex, to organize myself as fanatically as I do when at my desk. When Matthieu Ricard had given me his vision of taking a mini-Sabbath in the skies, I'd assumed that this was something available to a monk who'd meditated for three decades in the Himalayas, and not the rest of us.

But the next time I was flying home—from New York to California—I tried to take a page out of my former seatmate's near-empty book. I didn't turn on my monitor. I didn't race through a novel. I didn't even consciously try to do nothing: when an idea came to me or I recalled something I had to do back home, I pulled out a notebook and scribbled it down. The rest of the time, I just let my mind go foraging—or lie down—like a dog on a wide, empty beach.

It was three a.m. on the wristwatch I hadn't reset when I arrived home, but I felt as clear and refreshed as when, in the hour before sleeping, I choose not to scroll through YouTube or pick up a book but simply turn off all the lights and let some music wash over me. When I awoke the next morning, I felt as new as the world I looked out upon.

6 Coming Back Home

With every return to Nowhere, one can begin to discern its features, and with them its possibilities, a little more clearly. The place has moods and seasons as rich as the pulsing, red-dirt spaces of Australia's outback, as varied as the clouds you can see in a James Turrell Skyspace. Very often, I'll sit for weeks composing a work such as this one, making an outline, a linear A-B-C guide. The longer I sit still, however, the more those logical structures get turned inside out, till something beyond me is propelling me out of NOWHERE down an entirely unexpected sequence of Q-C-A. I think of the time when I was on a boat in the Pacific and a biologist set up a device that allowed us to hear what was going on beneath us. Under the still blue waters, it turned out, was an uproar as scratchily cacophonous as Grand Central Station at rush hour. Stillness has nothing to do with settledness or stasis.

"One of the strange laws of the contemplative life," Thomas Merton, one of its sovereign explorers, pointed out, "is that in it you do not sit down and solve problems: you bear with them until they somehow solve themselves. Or until life solves them for you." Or, as Annie Dillard, who sat still for a long time at Tinker Creek—and in many other places—has it, "I do not so much write a book as sit up with it, as with a dying friend."

It's only by taking myself away from clutter and distraction that I can begin to hear something out of earshot and recall that listening is much more invigorating than giving voice to all the thoughts and prejudices that anyway keep me company twenty-four hours a day. And it's only by going nowhere—by sitting still or letting my mind relax—that I find that the thoughts that come to me unbidden are far fresher and more imaginative than the ones I consciously seek out. Setting an autoresponse on my e-mail, turning off the TV when I'm on the treadmill, trying to find a quiet place in the midst of a crowded day (or city)—all quickly open up an unsuspected space.

•   •   •

It takes courage, of course, to step out of the fray, as it takes courage to do anything that's necessary, whether tending to a loved one on her deathbed or turning away from that sugarcoated doughnut. And with billions of our global neighbors in crying need, with so much in every life that has to be done, it can sound selfish to take a break or go off to a quiet place. But as soon as you do sit still, you find that it actually brings you closer to others, in both understanding and sympathy. As the meditative video artist Bill Viola notes, it's the man who steps away from the world whose sleeve is wet with tears for it.

In any case, few of us have the chance to step out of

our daily lives often, or for very long; Nowhere has to become somewhere we visit in the corners of our lives by taking a daily run or going fishing or just sitting quietly for thirty minutes every morning (a mere 3 percent of our waking hours). The point of gathering stillness is not to enrich the sanctuary or mountaintop but to bring that calm into the motion, the commotion of the world.

Indeed, Nowhere can itself often become a routine, a treadmill, the opposite of something living, if you don't see it as a way station: sometimes during his days on Mount Baldy, Leonard Cohen would get into his car, drive down from the mountain, and stop off for a Filet-O-Fish at McDonald's. Then, suitably fortified, he'd go back to his house in one of the more forgotten parts of central Los Angeles and stretch out in front of *The Jerry Springer Show* on TV.

After a day or two, having gotten the restlessness out of his system—and recalling, perhaps, why he'd wanted to go up the mountain in the first place—he would drive back, but never with a view to staying there forever. Though always faithful to his friend Sasaki, who lived to 107, Cohen had begun traveling to Mumbai to hear a retired bank manager talk about the place behind our self-contradictory ideas where notions of "you" and "me" dissolve; he'd taken to writing about traffic jams and Babylon again, and, fleeing every pretense of unworldliness or sanctity, he'd gone back full-time into the modest home he shares with his daughter and taken on a beautiful young companion.

At the age of seventy-three, Cohen launched a global concert tour that continued for six years, taking him from Hanging Rock in Australia to Ljubljana, from Saskatoon to Istanbul. He gave more than three hundred concerts in all, nearly every one lasting more than three hours.

I went to see him onstage as the tour began and felt as if the whole spellbound crowd was witnessing something of the monastery, the art that stillness deepens. Much of the time the singer stood motionless near the back of the stage, hat doffed, almost invisible, as if back in the meditation hall. Other times he was all but down on his knees, squeezing every last drop out of each confession or prayer. It was a remarkable thing to see a man in his midseventies summon such stillness and furious energy, such collectedness and openness about his longings and his panic.

In 2012, something even stranger happened: a new record came out with the decidedly unsexy title of *Old Ideas*. Nearly all the songs on it were slow to the point of being stationary and dealt with darkness or suffering or the leaden heart of a man who's "got no taste for anything at all." As with most of the singer's recent albums, all the tunes were really about death, saying good-bye not just to a young woman but to everything he loved, not least life itself.

One day I woke up in a hotel in the LA Live entertainment zone, a glittery new complex of singles bars and megascreens, high-rising towers and a concert hall. I went downstairs to collect my morning Awake tea and heard, from the album being featured in the coffeehouse that week, a seventy-seven-year-old Zen monk croaking about "going home" to a place that sounded very much like death.

Old Ideas, rather astonishingly, had gone to the top of the charts already in seventeen countries and hit the Top Five in nine others. The singer's cold and broken "Hallelujah" had recently occupied the number one, number two, and number thirty-six spots in the British Top 40 simultaneously and become the fastest-selling download in European history. Long past what looked like retirement age, Leonard Cohen had suddenly become the latest thing, the prince of fashion, once again.

Why were people across the planet reaching out for such a funereal album with such an antitopical title? I wondered. Maybe they were finding a clarity and wisdom in the words of someone who'd gone nowhere, sitting still to look at the truth of the world and himself, that they didn't get from many other recording artists? Cohen seemed to be bringing us bulletins from somewhere more rooted than the CNN newsroom, and to be talking to us, as the best friends do, without varnish or evasion or design. And why were so many hastening to concerts delivered by a monk in his late seventies? Perhaps they longed to be taken back to a place of trust—which is what Nowhere is, at heart—where they could speak and listen with something deeper than their social selves and be returned to a penetrating intimacy.

In an age of speed, I began to think, nothing could be more invigorating than going slow.

In an age of distraction, nothing can feel more luxurious than paying attention.

And in an age of constant movement, nothing is more urgent than sitting still.

You can go on vacation to Paris or Hawaii or New Orleans three months from now, and you'll have a tremendous time, I'm sure. But if you want to come back feeling new—alive and full of fresh hope and in love with the world—I think the place to visit may be Nowhere.

ACKNOWLEDGMENTS

I'm deeply happy and honored to be involved in one of the first TED Originals; I fell into the TED orbit barely a year ago and instantly felt I was among bright, fun, and deeply committed kindred spirits who saw all kinds of fresh ways for bringing our world to new life. I owe heartfelt thanks to Chris Anderson and Bruno Giussani at TED for bringing me into the fold, and to all the others who have worked so hard to build a community, advance a vision, throw a terrific party, and share ideas we might not otherwise get to hear.

In the context of this book, I owe especial thanks to June Cohen, one of TED's longtime inspirations, and to my editor, Michelle Quint, for bringing such invigorating enthusiasm and such a beautifully clarifying and tenacious eye to my every comma. I would also like to thank Susan Lehman, who originally came up with the idea for this book (and who regularly seems to know what I should be writing about even when I do not), and Benjamin Holmes, for his meticulous and sympathetic copyedit. It was amazing to have Chip Kidd, a longtime colleague and friend from afar, bring his inimitable eye and vision to our cover, while Eydís Einarsdóttir's images from one of my favorite places on earth deepened and illuminated the atmosphere I was trying to catch in my text.

I always owe huge thanks to my steadfast, brilliant friend and agent, Lynn Nesbit, and to Michael Steger at Janklow & Nesbit, for looking out for me—for all of us—in ways so human, so discerning, and so kind. And it must be clear how much I owe various friends and inspirations, some of them (Proust and Thoreau, Thomas Merton and Emily Dickinson) never quite met in the flesh, some of them (Leonard Cohen and Annie Dillard, Matthieu Ricard and the Fourteenth Dalai Lama) glimpsed here and there.

Thank you, finally, to the monks and oblates and fellow wanderers who pass through the New Camaldoli Hermitage, so open and forbearing even though I regularly do so little justice to their lives.

The images in this book were all taken by Icelandic/Canadian photographer Eydís S. Luna Einarsdóttir. They have not been digitally altered, beyond standard color correction.

Einarsdóttir began her visual journey at a young age, influenced by her father—an avid photographer—her artist mother, and the Icelandic light and landscape. Detail, contrast, and simplicity best describe her photography. Her subtle grasp of color and talent for lighting create an alluring and visually distinctive edge.

ARTIST'S STATEMENT

Stillness, or, in Icelandic, *kyrrð*—the word itself brings me right back to one of the few places I have ever found perfect stillness in mind and body: Iceland.

Every year I travel from my home in Vancouver, Canada, to Iceland, the place of my birth. I don't stay in the city much; instead, I head out to my parents' quiet lakeside cabin to take a rest from the self-imposed stress of my life and to experience *kyrrð og ró* (peace and quiet).

After a couple of days of recuperation, my parents and I head out on excursions around the island. To me these travels are not so much a photographic exploration as a time to visit with my parents and my "old" country; the camera simply comes along. However, with the breathtaking views and beautiful light Iceland offers, a stop here and there is inevitable.

As soon as I take out my camera I find that stillness within, that deep sense of peace that I crave every day. I get lost in such a beautiful way that it's hard to describe; it's as though I find a piece of me that I had lost without really knowing that I lost it. As I sit quietly looking through the viewfinder, my senses become heightened. The smell of the earth makes me feel grounded; the sound of waves crashing or grass rustling in the wind or the bleating of a lone sheep in the distance makes me feel so alive; and the vastness of what I see makes me feel expansive. This is what it is like to be in the Now, which is really just to be still in mind and body. My photographs come from a place of emotion. They are not an attempt to capture the perfect image, but to capture the feeling I experience as I witness the things in front of me.

ABOUT THE AUTHOR

PICO IYER has been traveling the world for more than forty years now, from Easter Island to Bhutan and Ethiopia to Los Angeles Airport. His descriptions of those journeys have appeared in such books as *Video Night in Kathmandu*, *The Lady and the Monk*, *The Global Soul*, and *The Open Road*, and he's written novels about Revolutionary Cuba and Islam. For twenty years he's been a constant contributor to *The New York Times*, *The New York Review of Books*, *Harper's*, *Time*, and scores of other magazines and newspapers across the globe. He currently serves as a Distinguished Presidential Fellow at Chapman University.

Pico Iyer's 14-minute talk, available for free at TED.com, is the companion to *The Art of Stillness*.

TED.com/stillness

PHOTO: JAMES DUNCAN DAVIDSON

RELATED TALKS ON TED.COM

Pico Iyer: *Where is home?*
go.ted.com/Iyer

More and more people worldwide are living in countries not considered their own. Pico Iyer—who himself has three or four "origins"—meditates on the joy of traveling and the meaning of home.

Carl Honore: *In praise of slowness*
go.ted.com/Honore

Journalist Carl Honore believes the Western world's emphasis on speed erodes health, productivity and quality of life. But there's a backlash brewing, as everyday people start putting the brakes on their all-too-modern lives.

Matthieu Ricard: *The habits of happiness*
go.ted.com/Ricard

What is happiness, and how can we all get some? Biochemist turned Buddhist monk Matthieu Ricard says we can train our minds in habits of well-being, to generate a true sense of serenity and fulfillment.

Louie Schwartzberg: *Nature. Beauty. Gratitude.*
go.ted.com/Schwartzberg

Louie Schwartzberg's stunning time-lapse photography—accompanied by powerful words from Benedictine monk Brother David Steindl-Rast—serves as a meditation on being grateful for every day.

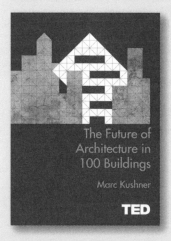

TED is a nonprofit devoted to spreading ideas, usually in the form of short, powerful talks (18 minutes or less) but also through books, animation, radio programs, and events. TED began in 1984 as a conference where Technology, Entertainment and Design converged, and today covers almost every topic—from science to business to global issues—in more than 100 languages.

TED is a global community, welcoming people from every discipline and culture who seek a deeper understanding of the world. We believe passionately in the power of ideas to change attitudes, lives and, ultimately, our future. On TED.com, we're building a clearinghouse of free knowledge from the world's most inspired thinkers—and a community of curious souls to engage with ideas and each other. Our annual flagship conference convenes thought leaders from all fields to exchange ideas. Our TEDx program allows communities worldwide to host their own independent, local events, all year long. And our Open Translation Project ensures these ideas can move across borders.

In fact, everything we do—from the TED Radio Hour to the projects sparked by the TED Prize, from TEDx events to the TED-Ed lesson series —is driven by this goal: How can we best spread great ideas?

TED is owned by a nonprofit, nonpartisan foundation.